dealing with
FAMILY
BREAK-UP

Kate Haycock

Wayland

Bullying

Eating Disorders

Relationships

Substance Abuse

Death

Family Break-up

Stress

Peer Pressure

Editor: Alison Cooper

Series editor: Deborah Elliott

Picture research: Liz Miller

Concept design: Joyce Chester

Book design: Helen White

First published in 1995 by

Wayland (Publishers) Ltd

61 Western Road, Hove,

East Sussex BN3 1JD

British Library Cataloguing in Publication
Data
Haycock, Kate
  Dealing with Family Break-up
  I. Title
  306.88

ISBN 0 7502 1642 5

Typeset by White Design
Printed and bound by Canale in Italy

All of the people who appear in the
photographs in this book are models.
Commissioned photographs arranged
by Zoë Hargreaves.

Contents

Why do families break up?

There are as many reasons for relationships and marriages breaking up as there are relationships and marriages. When people get married or move in together, they usually start with the best intentions. They are in love with each other and want to be happy. Sadly, a variety of circumstances can damage their relationship beyond repair and they may decide to split up.

In recent years divorce has become more and more common. One reason for this may be that people's expectations are greater today than they were in the past. Many people travel, leave the area they were brought up in, change jobs regularly. They want their lives to be enjoyable and fulfilling and sometimes they cannot achieve this with their partners.

Divorce is also much more acceptable than it was when our grandparents got married. Even twenty years ago, divorce was difficult to obtain, and couples put up with miserable marriages rather than suffer the scandal of getting divorced. It is possible that the number of divorces today is a truer reflection of how many relationships go wrong.

When parents decide to split up, children are the bystanders – they are not involved in the decision, although it dramatically affects their lives, both immediately and in the future. Understanding why your parents have decided that they cannot stay together is very difficult. If they love you, then why has one walked out? Why haven't they tried harder to stay together for your sake and for the sake of your brothers and sisters?

Money and economic pressures are common causes of family break-up. The rise in the standard of living means that people want more possessions and work harder to pay for them. This can leave them with less time and energy to devote to their partners and families. In many families both parents need to work to provide enough income to live on but they can find juggling work with bringing up children very difficult. Unemployment can also put a huge strain on a couple's relationship.

◀ **It can be very hard to understand why your parents are splitting up. You may feel very angry and let down, perhaps even a bit scared.**

▲ When a couple are already having problems, financial difficulties can be the final straw, causing a complete breakdown.

Michelle's parents moved around a lot. Her father was always starting new jobs, and she and her older sister, Anita, went to lots of different schools. Her mother went along with all this, but kept hoping that one day they would settle down in one place, where the children could go to the same school and they could all make longer-lasting friendships.

One day Michelle's father decided to buy a hotel and convert it into flats. He borrowed a lot of money. By the time the flats were ready, the property market had collapsed and so no one wanted to buy them. He became bankrupt. They had to sell everything. This was the last straw for Michelle's mum.

The strain of following her husband everywhere had been too much for her. She decided she wanted to split up. There was not much arguing.

Sometimes one or both of the partners meet someone else and fall in love with them. At this stage they may realize they made a big mistake with the person they married and decide that they would be much happier living with someone else.

Sometimes both partners realize that they are not compatible. They may have got married or moved in together in a hurry, perhaps because the woman was already pregnant. When they get down to the practical business of living together, they find many ways in which they are different.

Unfortunately relationships can break down because of violence to one of the partners or even to the children. Although this often seems an obvious sign for the victimized person to leave, this can often be a very difficult and frightening thing to do. It may take a long time and a lot of misery before that person feels ready or strong enough to walk out.

Parents usually want to do the best they possibly can for their children, but it is a hard job to do well. No one has any training for it. When different personalities live in a close environment together, clashes and strains are almost inevitable. A divorce or relationship breakdown is always painful and difficult; if children are involved, it hurts more people and everyone takes longer to adjust. Family break-up can have long-term psychological effects on the children.

▼ **Having a baby is a stressful event, as well as an exciting one, and it can put great strain on the parents' relationship.**

▶ A family break-up is difficult to deal with at any age and it can take the children involved a long while to recover.

Warren, now twenty, explains how he felt when his parents split up.

'When I was younger, my mum and dad were always fighting. Actually it was my dad, he used to drink a lot and get really mad. I know he used to hit my mum. It was really awful. So, to be honest, I wanted him to leave. I hated him. I just wanted our home to be peaceful again, and I wanted my mum to be free of his violence.

'When they told us he was leaving, I was so happy. I didn't want to see him for a long time, although he did visit. It's only now, years later, that I have any kind of relationship with him.'

While parents are going through the messy business of separation or divorce and sorting out the financial arrangements, the children can often be overlooked. Their cares, concerns, fears and sadness are often glossed over. They are left wondering why everything seems to have gone wrong and uncertain about what will happen to them. This book tries to help the children understand and cope with the situation in which they find themselves.

Is it my fault?

The time when your parents are breaking up can be a very confusing one. You may have experienced a long period of arguments and tension, but you will, in most cases, be hoping that your parents can sort it out and will eventually be happier together again. Or you may expect that this situation of constant rowing will continue, but at least you will still have both your parents around.

Then suddenly they tell you that it is over. They cannot live together any more. They explain that they have tried everything and have both decided it is for the best. Your whole world is shattered.

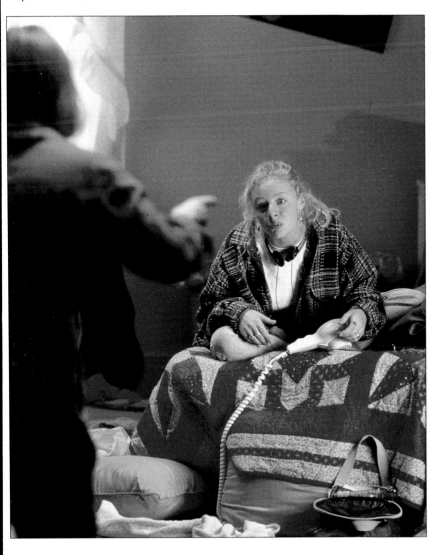

◀ **Arguments with parents are common when you are in your teens. If your parents split up, it's easy to start blaming yourself for having made their lives more difficult.**

You instinctively feel that you could have tried harder. Maybe you could have been better behaved, sulked less, tidied your room more often. Then maybe mum and dad would not be so fed up, so tired, so unhappy.

'My first thought was that it was my fault. I remembered all the times my mum and dad asked me and my brother to do something and we didn't. We moaned or shouted, and they told us we were naughty and ungrateful. If only we had tried harder to be what they wanted none of this would have happened.'

This reaction is very common. You are in a state of shock. You struggle to understand the situation but find that you cannot make head nor tail of it. Perhaps this is because your parents have not explained it to you clearly enough, but even if they have, you still find it desperately difficult to make sense of what is happening.

It is very natural to feel guilty or responsible. Because of the pain and distress they have been going through, your parents are bound to be more short-tempered with you, and less patient. This

only makes you feel all the more that you are somehow to blame. They have not been able to show you love and approval, so you feel that they do not love you and you start looking for reasons for this – you are not well-behaved enough, or grateful enough. That last school report, that must be why they are upset with you. You have let them down. You are a disappointment. You have failed to live up to their expectations.

Don't fall into this trap – you are no different from any other child. In families that seem perfectly happy (and very few have no

Gabrielle was eleven when she noticed things changing between her parents. Her father was away working more and more, and her mother made the odd snide comment like 'I thought for once he'd try to make it home on time'.

She heard them arguing, but only behind closed doors. She heard her name mentioned a lot and wondered what was going to happen. Her father finally left home, and her mother refused to discuss it. She felt it was somehow her fault. Maybe she'd upset her father and he felt they were both ganging up on him.

problems at all), children demand things of their parents and are often less than perfectly behaved. You are just behaving naturally.

The important thing to remember is that your parents' love for you is different from their love for each other. Their love for you is unconditional – they brought you into the world, with no expectations of you. You didn't ask to be born. But when two people enter into a relationship each expects something of the other. Often one feels that he or she is expected to give more than the other, and may feel taken for granted, or unappreciated. They feel they are having to change, or forget their own wishes or plans, for the other person.

So your parents can stop loving each other, but they will not stop loving you. They may show it in a different way if they are going through a difficult time, or they may scarcely be able to show it at all. They may be feeling unloved themselves, and so find it hard to give love to anyone else.

Although it is difficult, try to keep showing them that you love them. They need all the help they can get at the moment, just like you do. Above all, remember that, if your parents do decide to split up, there is nothing you can do to stop them. It is something they have to decide between them.

Lydia was afraid that it was her fault her dad had left.

'When my mum told me that my dad was moving out, I felt really guilty. I knew they had been having money problems, and I thought, it's probably my fault for always wanting new clothes and stuff.

'I really worried about that for quite a while – a couple of months – but when things quietened down a bit, I eventually talked to both of them about why they split up, and I realized it was nothing to do with me. That made me feel a lot better.'

▼ **When parents split up, it is not because they are disappointed in their children, but often because they feel let down by each other.**

What does it feel like?

It is impossible to describe all the different feelings that the children of separating parents go through. Your initial feelings will not be the same as those that you feel after a few days or weeks, and months and years later you will still be experiencing emotions connected with the events that took place.

It is very common to have mixed feelings. If there has been a period of arguing and tension in the home, you may feel relieved that this is finally over, but you will also be sad that your parents have not been able to resolve their differences, or angry that they have 'failed' you as parents.

Shock

'I didn't have any reaction at all. I suppose I was in shock. I just felt completely numb all over. I didn't want to move, eat, do anything, talk to anyone. It was very strange.'

When a major event happens suddenly in a person's life, shock is often the initial reaction. It is a very difficult emotion or response to describe, as it can take on many different forms. There may be a feeling of disbelief, and people often find that they go numb. Your whole body may

▲ **Shock can make you feel numb and totally cut-off from the normal life that is going on around you.**

seize up and you may just want to sit or lie still. You may not want, or feel able, to talk to anyone. This is perfectly OK. No one should expect you to do anything you don't want to at this time.

If you do not have the reaction which you expect or which is expected of you, you may feel guilty that you are not more upset. Don't feel bad. You cannot help how you react. Often this initial reaction is your body's defence system – to protect you at a difficult time.

Sadness

'I cried and cried and cried. I couldn't stop. I just felt so unhappy. I kept thinking about all the happy times we had had together and how they were over forever.'

You are experiencing a huge change in your life. You feel lost, alone, and often desperately unhappy. The most natural thing in the world is to grieve when something so serious happens. Your parents splitting up is one of the biggest upsets you can have.

▼ **It can be very hard to 'put on a brave face' when you are feeling so upset.**

Crying helps. If you can cry, you will at least feel you are releasing a lot of the emotion which you feel inside. It is very exhausting, but you should never try to stop yourself crying. You should spend this time indulging in your emotions. Do not feel that you have to carry on as before and put on a brave face – your school work can wait, your friends, dance classes, football training and so on will all still be there in a few weeks' time. In the end you will feel better, because you have let your emotions come to the outside and can then start to deal with them.

Anger

'I was so angry with my father for leaving. I hated him. I couldn't believe he could be so selfish as to leave. It was all right for him going off to a new life.'

If you feel angry, that is hardly surprising. You feel let down by the two most important people in your life. You have been hurt, through no fault of your own. Why has this happened to you? Why you and not one of the other hundreds of children at school? What have you done to deserve this? It all seems very unfair at the moment and you will feel like

expressing your anger and frustration at the situation. You may want to shout or argue. You may want to kick something, hit someone, throw something. Remember, though, you are not the only one. There are hundreds of thousands of children, and older people, who are going through or have gone through a similar experience to the one you are going through now. This may not be much consolation, but knowing that they will all come through it, and that you will come through it too, is something to hang on to in these unhappy times.

Unfortunately, some less sympathetic people may get annoyed with you if you show your anger. They may try to tell you to calm down, but how are you supposed to calm down, when you have all these feelings churning around inside you? Remember that it is natural for you to feel angry. You will 'calm down' eventually, in your own time, as your anger subsides. One way of getting rid of your anger in the meantime is to do something physical – go swimming, take the dog for a walk, go running, play sport. It releases physical energy and also makes you feel tired, which will help you to sleep more peacefully.

◄ **Exercise is a good way to get rid of anger and tension.**

▲ You may find that you can't concentrate on school work or on your job because you are constantly worrying about what is going to happen to you.

Fear

'My first thought was, "Now, what's going to happen?" I'm really worried that we're going to move out of the house to somewhere else, and I'll have to change school, and lose all my friends.'

Change is a major source of stress, and one reason for this is the fear of the unknown. Perhaps you know that there is going to be a change but no one has sat down and asked you what you want to do, or explained what the plans are. Not knowing how things are going to change is very unsettling, particularly when you are used to a routine, seeing the same people and coming home to the same house every day, and generally feeling that your life has some permanence to it.

When this is suddenly thrown into doubt, you start worrying. What is my life going to be like now? Where am I going to live? Will we have enough money? Am I still going to see mum or dad? What about my brothers and sisters – are we all going to live together? What about my school work – I don't feel I can concentrate now and I'm worried about my exams?

It is perfectly all right to ask questions. Maybe your parents do not know exactly what is going to happen either, but they probably have more of an idea than you do.

Denial

'I just kept hoping that, if I waited long enough, mum and dad would sort out their differences and get back together again. That's what I want more than anything in the world.'

It is very common to have trouble accepting that your parents are getting divorced and many young people deny it for months, or even years. You may refuse to accept the fact, clinging to the belief that it is only a temporary situation; it will resolve itself eventually, your parents will get back together, and you will all be able to be a happy family again.

▲ **Many couples go to a counsellor to try to sort out their problems. They only decide to split up if all their efforts to save their relationship have failed.**

It is rare, though, for a couple to decide, after a period of time, to get back together again. Usually parents agonize for a very long time before deciding to split up in the first place. Although it may be painful for you, it is much more realistic to try to accept the break-up as final. Then you can begin the slow process of getting used to it.

Parents have feelings too

Sometimes when they are going through difficult times themselves, your parents may not show their love and care for you in the same way as they might if they were not under strain.

When their relationship fails, your parents' behaviour may seem very strange. They may appear distant or fraught. It is easy to feel disappointed, upset, angry or ashamed of them. You may feel that this situation is their fault, that they have brought the problem on themselves. You did not ask them to split up – although if your family life was unhappy maybe you feel it is for the best.

It is important to realize that your parents are not doing what they are doing to hurt you deliberately or to ruin your life, although you may sometimes feel that they are. They may have taken a long time to decide to separate, but when it actually happens, and they are left on their own, they might feel a great sense of shock. They can't believe what they have done.

▶ **'You've ruined my life...'**
It's normal to feel angry with
your parents but bear in
mind that they too might feel
their lives have been ruined.

Your parents have been used to sharing their life; now they have to face it on their own. It seems a daunting task, and doubt starts creeping in. Maybe, they think, they were better off before – after all they did have some good times. They begin to forget the misery they felt before. Maybe they should just have had a break and tried really hard to work at their relationship – it could have been all right.

Parents whose partners have left them will be dealing with feelings of rejection, especially if the partner is having a relationship with someone else. They will feel hurt, alone and empty, and may find it hard to show you the love they feel. All the things which you have experienced – shock, sadness, fear, guilt – they will be feeling too. They will also be feeling guilty about what they have done to you.

People who are used to having someone else around to lean on, turn to, even moan at, need to become accustomed to being on their own. It takes some people longer than others to cope with change. Most eventually do cope, but it takes patience on all sides.

Many parents feel a sense of alarm that they have made such a mess of their own lives. They worry greatly that they are unfit to be parents. Try not to give them a hard time. Try not to test them – although this may seem difficult.

Remember that your parents are going through a lot too. They may be tense and suffering from lack of sleep. This may make them less tolerant, more irritable. Your demands, which to you seem small, may become too much. Even asking questions may make them feel on edge. Don't stop asking questions – just try to choose a moment when your mum or dad is not worrying about a hundred-and-one other things.

◄ **Your parent has to come to terms with the loss of someone they once loved, or may still love. You might find it difficult to feel much sympathy, but try to understand the pain she or he may be feeling.**

seemed she wasn't really listening to what he had to say. He felt as if he was banging his head against the wall, trying to make her interested in what he was talking about.

Luis felt that he was being as helpful and supportive as he could. He didn't moan about the lack of proper meals, and tried to chat to his mum. He couldn't figure out why she wasn't the same as she used to be.

'Although I felt sorry for my mum, I felt I had problems too. I missed my dad and had to get used to living with just my mum. And I was coping with other things - career choices, girlfriends, that sort of thing.

'All the time I'd been growing up, I'd expected my parents to be there for me. Now, at a time when I really needed their attention and support, they didn't seem to be there for me. Often I felt my mum was humouring me.'

Luis's mum was in a state of shock. The first thing she felt she had to do was to throw herself into her work, because that was her only real source of security. The sooner she got started, the better. She felt a sense of panic about the future and about having to cope with Luis. She had to make all the decisions about him on her own and make sure he wasn't at a disadvantage because his father wasn't around. All these things kept her awake for hours at night.

Worrying as she was about all the practical things, she ended up not spending any time listening to Luis - her mind was always on the next thing she had to sort out.

Luis's mum and dad had separated and his dad had moved out. His mum spent a lot of time crying on her own. Luis really missed his dad - they used to do the football pools together and talk about TV programmes they had watched. Mum wasn't interested in the same things. He felt deserted by his dad, and although he felt sorry for his mum, she just wasn't so much fun.

His mum was working hard again now, and often there was not much to eat in the house. He would come home to an empty house and look in the kitchen cupboards - nothing. So he'd go out to the chip shop and buy himself some chips. Then he'd come home and not really feel like starting on his homework, so he'd ring up his friends to pass the time.

His mum seemed to be very jumpy. Half the time she'd be trying to please him, and half the time it

Like most parents in her situation, Luis's mother was only worrying about him and about their future, and she wanted to do her best for him. Although Luis felt let down for a while, after a few months things started to get better. His mother got more used to her new life and began to accept it. She became more relaxed, and they even talked about how it had been during those first few, hard months.

Your parents are not superhuman. They may know, for example, that they shouldn't run down their ex-partner, your mother or father, in front of you, but at times they will be feeling fed up or angry and will simply not be able to bite their tongue. We do not always act rationally. When our emotions run riot, it is difficult to check our behaviour in advance. It is hard to accept, but it is a period of adjustment for all of you.

▲ **Feelings of hurt, anger and rejection may make it impossible for your mum or dad to hold back from complaining about your other parent.**

▶ **If your parents start arguing whenever they meet, tell them how difficult and distressing this is for you.**

Learning to cope

In the initial stages of a family break-up, everyone's emotions are in turmoil. No one can think clearly about how to proceed, and each member of the family has expectations and needs which the others cannot fulfil.

How do people cope? At times, it seems you are never going to come through it. You feel your whole life is a mess and will never be the same again. Well, that is certainly true – how can it be when you have gone through such a huge upset to your life? But it will get better, and you will get over this rough patch.

You learn – as we all do – how to cope. Most of us are survivors, and these experiences are all part of life. As we learn to deal with difficult times, so we develop as people and cope better with what life throws at us later on.

Caught in the middle
'What I really hated was my dad didn't like me to talk about my mum at all. I found that really upsetting – I mean, it was like she didn't exist any more, just because he didn't see her.'

If your mum or dad behaves like this, it is probably because she or he is so angry and hurt. Try to be sensitive to your parent's feelings, especially just after the break-up. The parent with whom you live may also feel aggrieved if you come home from visiting your other parent full of stories about where you have been and the presents that have been bought for you. If he or she is working hard to look after you, your behaviour may seem very ungrateful, although you may not intend it to be like that. Remember to try to be tactful.

'My mother tries to make me feel uncomfortable seeing my dad. She seems to forget sometimes that I didn't divorce him – that was her decision. I still want to see him as much as ever – unfortunately, I can't, but at least when I do, she should let me enjoy it without giving me a hard time.'

Your parent should not make you feel bad for seeing your other parent, or even worse, prevent you from seeing your mum or dad at all, unless of course you are prevented from doing so by the courts. You have a right and a need to see both parents. It is best for you to be able to carry on as normally as possible, and missing one of your parents will not help you at this difficult time.

Sometimes your parents might try to get you to take sides or pass messages between them. Try not to let this happen. It will make you feel disloyal, and that you are being used by them to get at each other.

Jean-Paul found himself caught up in his parents' squabbles.

'I felt like a piggy in the middle and it was really awful, because I love both my parents, and thought they were stupid for quarrelling all the time, even though they had split up. Eventually I told my grandma about it, and she talked to my mum and said I was really fed up with the way they played me off against each other.

'It was great because my mum listened to her, and realized that it was time to stop feeling bitter, and to try to get on with her life. Things have really changed now and, although they don't see each other, when they have to sort something out, usually to do with me, they do it on the phone and it's actually quite civilized.'

▲ **Your parents may think they are protecting you by not discussing the break-up with you. They may not be aware of your need to know what is going on.**

'Talk to me...'

You may be confused and angry because you feel that you have been left out of any decisions about the family and the future. You may feel that you have lots of questions but do not know who can answer them.

When your parents are breaking up, they are probably going through such a hard time that they do not stop to think about what you feel or how much you understand. To them, it may be perfectly obvious why they are breaking up, and what is going to happen to the family now, so they wrongly assume that it is obvious to you too.

This is a common problem in human communication. Each person thinks that the other should know what they are thinking, so nobody says anything, and they never sort anything out. It is therefore important to voice your concerns and ask questions. Persist if you don't get the answers straightaway – then your parents will realize that there are lots of things on your mind. They may think they are protecting you by not telling you very much. If you keep asking questions, then they will realize that you need to have explanations.

Make sure that you pick a suitable moment – not when your mother is rushing around getting ready for work, or when your father has just had a bad meeting with the bank manager. If you are not sure how to start, say something like, 'Mum (or Dad), there are some things that have been bothering me.' Hopefully she or he will then ask what is worrying you and you can start to explain.

Looking for comfort

When your parents break up, it can be a real comfort to have someone else around. If you have sisters or brothers, you may feel a lot less lonely, even if you don't have much in common. Relatives and neighbours can also help. If you are lucky, your grandparents may live close by, so there is always somewhere to go when you are sad or miserable.

It may really help to talk to other people of your own age who have gone through a family break-up or are doing so at the moment. Just knowing that someone else is in the same situation as you makes you feel less of an outsider, and you can share your experiences with someone who understands. It's also comforting to find that people do recover.

Carlton was extremely upset when his parents split up.

'It came as a total shock, I just couldn't get used to the idea. Then one day one of the boys in my class came in really late and had really bloodshot eyes. I asked him what was the matter and he said that his parents had been fighting all night, and that they always did.

'I told him my parents had just split up, and we got talking about it. I felt much better just telling someone who knew what I was on about, and so did he. We're really good friends now, and it's really helped us both get through everything.'

Catherine's parents split up when she was eleven, and afterwards she lived with her mum. At the time of the break-up, her parents were often too preoccupied, tense or tired to spend much time with her.

Catherine's grandfather lived on his own up the road, and Catherine used to go to see him nearly every day. She loved his house, and she used to sit and tell him all about her day and what she had done at school. When she was upset, she would often burst out crying when she saw him. He would listen to her and give her tea and biscuits and make her feel much better. Then he would tell her stories about him and her grandma which would make her laugh, and she used to forget completely that she had been so fed up.

Her grandfather's support really helped Catherine to cope with what had happened.

Personal problems

Adjusting to having only one parent around can be really hard when you are in your teens. You might find it difficult to talk to the parent of the opposite sex about personal problems and the physical changes you are experiencing – either because you are embarrassed, or because your parent is.

Fathers often do not feel qualified to help their daughters on 'women's issues'. They probably worry about this but do not know how to do anything about it – so they just hope the problem will go away. Mothers too can feel at a loss to know what to say to their sons. If you are finding this situation difficult, try talking to a sympathetic relative, your doctor, or perhaps the parent of a close friend.

Keeping in touch

It can be very upsetting when you lose touch with one of your parents. Maybe he or she walked out and has not wanted any contact. It may be some time before you feel you would like to make contact, but if it is something you really want to do then persist, even if it is difficult and causes rows. Perhaps you could write, or telephone him or her. Discuss it with the parent you live with, or with a grandparent, aunt or uncle from that parent's family. Your parents may not speak to each other any more, but may not mind you making your own arrangements. It is natural to want to keep contact with both your parents, despite what has happened in the past.

▶ **'Dear Dad...' It's all-too-easy to lose contact with the parent who has left home, especially if you think your other parent will be upset if you attempt to make contact.**

Meredith and her younger brother live with her dad. She feels that she misses out more than her brother does by not having her mum around.

'Dad never discusses anything to do with periods or boyfriends or anything – I suppose he thinks I'll talk to people at school about it. It doesn't really bother me. I guess it bothers him more than me. It just makes me wish I had a mum around. And it makes things a bit awkward between me and dad – I mean, we were really close when I was little, but we're sort of growing apart now.'

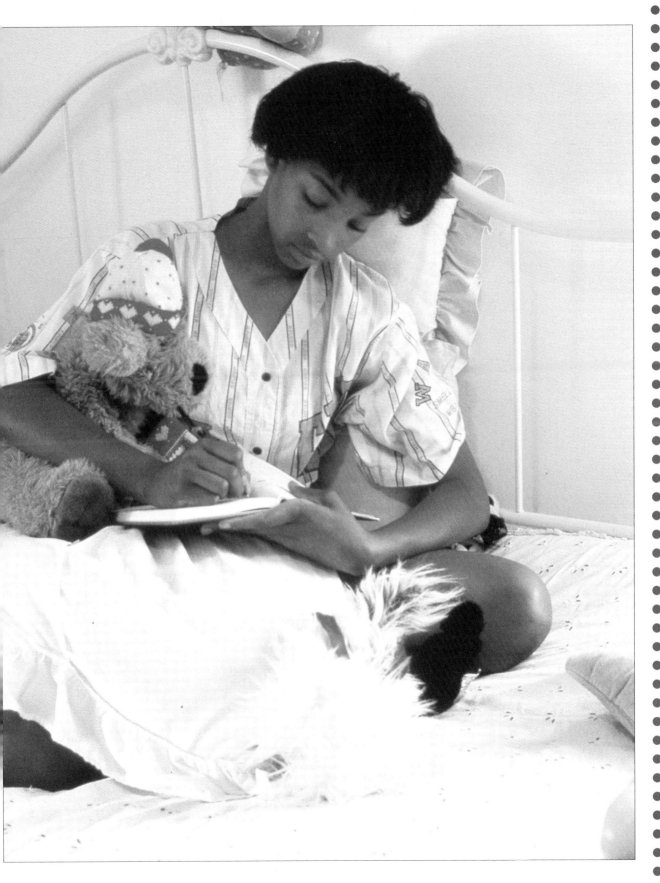

Facing the world

When your parents decide to split up, you may find that you not only have to adjust emotionally to the new situation, but also have to deal with practical changes and the reaction of people outside the immediate family.

What will people think?

Scott was ashamed to tell anyone that his parents were getting divorced.

'I was really worried that people would think differently of me if they knew. I didn't know how to answer people's questions.

'Eventually I decided it was best to be honest – just giving straight answers. My friends at school didn't really mention it after that, and I realized it was not such a big deal to them as I had thought.'

◀ **You may not want to tell your friends that your parents have split up, but, if you do, you might find some have been through the same experience themselves.**

You may feel embarrassed about the situation, but it is not your fault that your parents have separated, and no one should think badly of you. You should try to be proud of your parents despite what has happened.

Even today there is a certain stigma attached to divorce, in some groups of society. Some older people, for example, still feel it is immoral to divorce, or that the couple should work harder at their relationship, staying together through thick and thin, even if both are miserable. In previous generations many people did stay together and were very unhappy. Today more people believe that this should not happen.

It is very upsetting to face disapproval but do not think that everyone in the world will react in this way. You will learn that there are many caring people around, who can help you, and who will not judge.

New houses, different schools
When your parents separate, you may face major upheavals, such as starting a different school or moving into a new house. If this happens, it is important to maintain something familiar in your life – even if you are in a new bedroom, having your own things around you can make you feel more secure. If you have a pet, maybe you can take it with you to your new home.

▲ **Finding your way around and making new friends all take time when you move to a different school.**

After their separation, Patricia split her time equally between her two parents' homes.

'It was strange, having two bedrooms. I still kept most of my things at mum's place - which was where we all used to live. For a while I didn't really feel like having any personal things in dad's house. But after a while, I decided to make it feel more homely - after all, I was spending half my time there.

'Dad let me paint it, so it felt more like my own room, rather than a guest room. I've got used to carrying bits and pieces between the two houses, and occasionally I forget something which is really annoying, but it's nice because I see both my parents equally.'

Money problems

One way in which your life can change quite dramatically is the amount of money available now that your parents are living apart.

Lack of money can be an additional strain after a break-up. While your parents sort things out and get back on their feet, you may have to be patient. Although it will be hard if your friends at school all have more new clothes than you, it's not the end of the world. Your parents will be trying to earn as much as they can, but then they will obviously have less time to spend with you, and will be more tired.

'My dad was really tired all the time. I knew he didn't sleep very well, and work was quite hard. He didn't get many of the household jobs done - I used to put the rubbish out, do the washing up, even do a lot of the cooking and cleaning. Now, he pays someone to help with the cleaning and ironing which makes things a lot easier around here.'

You shouldn't be expected to shoulder the burden of keeping the household going – there's plenty of time for that when you get older! If you are having to help out a lot, and you feel it is unreasonable, tell your parent. Maybe he or she has not realized that you have no time to go out with your friends or to do your school work.

Arguments about money are also common. You may feel that you are caught in the middle of your parents' bitterness about how the financial side of their relationship has been settled. If so, tell them that it is unfair of them to involve you in this.

Barbara lived in a large house before her parents split up, but it has now been sold and Barbara is living in a small flat with her mother.

'It's not nearly as nice as our old place. We had to find it in a hurry, and mum has tried to make it like home. She says it's only until she can get on her feet, and then we'll get a better place.

'Also, she has to work full time now to pay for everything. She worked part time for years, so now she has to get her career going again. When I get home from school, I get my own tea and start my homework before she gets back.

'She's always tired - she comes in, does a few jobs around the flat and then collapses in front of the TV. I don't think she's got a very well-paid job, so I know there's not going to be much money for a while. I'm going to get a part-time job as soon as I'm old enough, so that I can afford to buy clothes and things for myself.'

Lauren found that her parents had very different attitudes to school work.

'My mum never let us watch TV until we had done our homework. But at my dad's we could do more or less whatever we liked. Mum got quite angry about it, and used to say that dad didn't care about our education. Fortunately we were all mature enough to realize that it was important to do our homework anyway, but it would have been really easy to take advantage of the situation, and refuse to accept mum's rules because dad didn't go along with them.'

Breaking the rules

Some young people find that the change in their situation affects their behaviour.

It is often difficult for one parent to maintain discipline after a break-up. He or she will be feeling guilty about what has happened and may not want to be too strict. You may feel that you have lost respect for your parents as role models and do not want to fall in with their set of rules. If you see your parents separately, you may find that they each have different rules, and that can be confusing. You may find yourself playing one off against the other.

▶ **It's very tempting to see how much you can get away with when you are living with only one parent.**

'I really rebelled for a while after my parents split up. My dad moved abroad, and my mother basically couldn't cope,' says Nelson, aged fifteen. 'I stayed out late, got involved with drink and drugs, and played truant from school a lot. Mum used to go mad at me, but the more she yelled, the worse I got.

'I think in retrospect I was angry at my dad for leaving, and tested my mum as far as I could. Of course, she was going through a lot herself and although I know she worried about me, she didn't feel she had any authority over me. After all, I'm taller than her, and my attitude was not really very approachable.'

Doing your own thing

Sometimes you will be torn between loyalty to your parents and your need to lead your own life. It is only natural that you will sometimes want to spend time doing things with friends and people of your own age. If you were living with both parents, you would have no problem about doing this, so although you may feel guilty, it is important to consider your own needs. Your parents will have to let you go eventually, so if you introduce the idea to them gradually, they will have time to get used to it.

◄ **It's natural to want to spend more time with people of your own age as you get older.**

Marianne's parents agreed that she would live with her mum but stay with her dad every second weekend.

'The problem was I sometimes got invited to friends' houses for Saturday night, and I actually preferred going there to staying with my dad. He really looked forward to my visits. I felt really torn and guilty about disappointing him. It took me ages to face up to him and tell him that I wasn't going to go there one weekend. At first he was hurt, but eventually he got used to it.'

A stepfamily

It can be very hard to accept that your parents no longer love each other, and getting used to living with only one of them may take a while. Stepfamilies can add to the difficulties of life after a break-up.

'My dad met someone else soon after my parents split up. I had got used to seeing him on his own, so I didn't like it much when Sheila always came along too. I mean, she tried hard to be nice, but I resented not having so much time with my dad.'

When your parent meets a potential new partner, he or she will naturally want to spend a lot of time with that person. Your mum or dad will be hoping that you will like the new person too, so that you can all do things together. You, on the other hand, may feel that you are not yet ready to get used to 'someone else' in your life. You are still adjusting to the new situation after the break-up. It is natural for you to be reluctant to welcome a stranger into your family.

It is important to remember that your parent's new partner is in a very difficult position. If he or she comes to live with you, you may resent him or her 'taking over' the household, especially if the old rules and routines are changed. You may feel he or she is taking your parent away from you, or you may feel that you are too old to accept a new 'mother' or 'father'. However reasonable the new partner tries to be, you think everything he or she does is wrong.

Carrie's father married again soon after he had split up with her mother. His new wife was a lot younger than her mum. She was quite friendly; in fact Carrie thought she was too friendly. She tried to confide in Carrie and talk to her about her dad: 'Oh, isn't it awful the way he tells those terrible jokes? '

Carrie was not impressed – who was this person trying to run down her father? She was quite naturally put off by her father's new wife's behaviour and became very defensive, refusing to have anything to do with her dad's wife.

▲ If you've enjoyed spending more time with your parent, it's not surprising that you feel a bit jealous, upset or resentful when a new partner comes along.

Sabrina was fourteen when her dad left and her mum found a new partner.

'I couldn't believe mum liked Tim more than my dad. I didn't like him at all. In fact I hated him and didn't want him to come to the house. Whenever he came I would just go to my room and stay there. Mum got really annoyed with me but I didn't care.'

She didn't like it at all when Tim actually moved in with them.

'I felt that I'd been through a non-stop period of change and upheaval. Now I was expected to get used to a new man living in the house. He moved in and acted as if it was his place.

'I just couldn't help comparing him with dad. He was quite friendly to me, and I suppose he felt uncomfortable not knowing where he stood with me, but it just took me ages to get used to it.

'The only thing that made me accept it was that my mum was much happier. If it made her happy, having him around, then at least that was better than before, when she was depressed and crying all the time.'

Stepbrothers and stepsisters

If your divorced or separated parent meets someone else, who is also divorced or separated and has children, the chances are that you are going to have to deal with stepbrothers and sisters. It will take time to get used to living with new people. As Pilar (below) found, it's very important to feel that you have a space where you can shut yourself away and be alone with your thoughts without anyone disturbing you.

It can be very difficult if you are expected to live with a stepfamily too soon after your parents have split up. But many people find that, once they get used to it, they can enjoy spending time with their stepfamily.

When Pilar's parents split up, her younger sister, Kara, stayed with her mum, while Pilar went to live with her dad. Everything was fine for a while. Pilar knew that her dad was seeing another woman, called Amanda, and had met her, but it came as a shock when her dad told her that Amanda and her two sons were coming to live with them too.

The sons were older than Pilar – one was fifteen and the other thirteen. Pilar was quite a quiet, studious child, but the boys, who had been through a family break-up themselves, were noisy and picked on Pilar, making her life at home a misery. Pilar became quite withdrawn and spent more time at friends' houses. At times she felt that her dad's house was no longer her home – she didn't want to go home.

Pilar eventually decided to tell her dad about it. She picked a time when they were alone in the house – which had become less and less often – and found he was quite understanding.

Although he didn't have much authority over the boys, he did introduce a rule that they could not go into Pilar's room under any circumstances. They teased her about it for a while but eventually they lost interest and stopped bothering her.

Before long Pilar felt happier about going home, because she knew she could shut herself in her room without worrying about her privacy being invaded.

Sometimes your parents may behave in ways which can be very hurtful. After her parents split up, Morag's father and his new wife bought a shop. Morag used to go and work there on Saturdays.

'One day, my dad told me, if anybody asked, to say I was his niece, as his wife didn't want anyone to ask any embarrassing questions. I felt horrible – like my father wasn't proud of me and wanted to disown me.

'I didn't tell anyone for a while, but eventually I confided in my older sister, who was outraged. She told me not to take it personally. She said it wasn't anything I had done, but that our dad and his new wife were feeling insecure and worried about what other people would think. They hadn't considered my feelings.

'I felt a lot better after talking about it, and managed to put it out of my mind. It still upset me when I thought about it, but I tried to think about all the people who did like me and said nice things to me. It made me pity my dad a bit in the end, because he wasn't able to love me like a daughter any more, because his wife was jealous of anyone else being in his life.'

▲ If your parents had an unhappy relationship and the situation at home was very difficult, you might find that life with your stepfamily is more enjoyable.

Life goes on

At the time of a family break-up, you may feel your whole life has been shattered. But, as we will see, people do survive. Some even feel that they have gained something positive from their experiences. The children of separated parents, for instance, often feel that they had to grow up quickly. Many think that their parents' separation made them become independent at an earlier age, and enabled them to cope better with life's problems.

▼ **Life after a break-up will never be the same. But that doesn't mean that things will never get better.**

wrapped up in his own problems and sorrow.

'My mother showed her love for my brother and me by working really hard to send us to good schools – she felt a good education was really important. In the end she took me to live with her in the Midlands – we had been living in Scotland until then – and I went to a new school.

'I just accepted everything that happened to me – I think you do when you are a child. But now I really feel I missed out on a childhood. Oh, I know they cared, but they just didn't seem to realize that I needed time and attention. I found out they were not as together as I had always thought and assumed they were. They started leaning on me for support – sharing their problems with me.

Shona's mother was very young when she married her father. After having two children, she started developing a life of her own outside the marriage and had a few affairs.

Shona often heard rows, and finally her dad told Shona and her brother that he and their mother were going to split up. Their mother was away at the time.

'I found it earth-shattering,' said Shona. 'Although my mum had been off doing her own thing a lot, it just came as such a shock. I thought things would really change – I was afraid I might not see my mother very much any more. The funny thing was, she came back that weekend and nothing actually changed on the surface. My mother still came to stay every weekend – as if to try and make a show of keeping the family together.

'We lived on a farm, and my father was really preoccupied with that, and although he treated me like his little girl, he had less time for me, and it didn't ever seem to occur to him that I was unhappy or confused. He seemed to be

'For a while I resented it. I felt I needed them to be proper, dependable parents to me, but now I am older I feel that it made me grow up more quickly. I recognize my parents are individuals. It is a very different relationship to what it was before, but it feels like we are more equal, and we appreciate each other more.'

Some young people, like Xanthe, speak positively of an arrangement where they split their time between their two parents.

'I actually enjoyed seeing my parents separately. We often used to find it difficult to agree on things, but now I do different things with my mum and with my dad. They make more of an effort to do things with me, like taking me ice-skating or to the cinema, and I make less of a fuss when they ask me to help out with chores and things like that. I feel I get the best of both worlds.

'I also spend more time with each of them on their own, and have got closer to them and know them better as people. Now that we have all adjusted to life after the break-up, I actually prefer it like this to how it was before.'

Stepfamilies can also have their positive side.

Tamsin's mother got married two years after her parents separated. A year later her mum had a new baby. Tamsin was delighted. 'It's so great having a little sister. We all really love her.

'My stepfather also had two kids. Although I found it hard at first living with a stepbrother and sister, we soon found that, because we had all been through a hard time while our parents were breaking up, we actually had a lot in common, and we all became good friends.

'I really like having a big family. I was an only child before.'

Do not believe anyone if they tell you that dealing with a family break-up is going to be easy. As you have seen from the stories in this book, many young people go through very difficult times, and it may sometimes seem that things are never going to get better. But eventually you and your parents will adjust to the new situation. In time, the new house, school, or even family, may seem as familiar as the old, and you will settle into a comfortable routine. So, take encouragement from all the people who have survived and are able to be positive about what has happened. Life does go on!

▼ **A family break-up is painful and traumatic, but once you recover from it, you might find life is better than it was before.**

Glossary

compatible Suited (to one another).

implications Possible results.

psychological Affecting the mind.

rejection Feeling unwanted, turned down.

snide Critical, unpleasant.

stigma Shame, disgrace.

stress Feeling under physical, emotional or mental pressure or strain.

unconditional Complete, unquestioning.

upheaval Change, disturbance.

victimized To punish someone or discriminate against them unfairly; to make them into victims.

Further reading

How it Feels when a Parent Dies by Jill Krementz (Victor Gollancz, 1986)
How it Feels when Parents Divorce by Jill Krementz (Victor Gollancz, 1984)
Juniper. A Mystery by Gene Kemp (Faber & Faber, 1986)
When Parents Split Up: Divorce Explained to Young People by Ann Mitchell (Chambers, 1986)

Acknowledgements

Thanks to the staff and pupils of Blatchington Mill School, Hove, East Sussex and to the following organizations which supplied the photographs used in this book: Cephas 32 (Jim Loring), 44 (Mick Rock); Eye Ubiquitous 35; Images Colour Library 37; Skjold 18, 27, 28; Tony Stone Worldwide 4-5 (Howard Grey), 6 (Jon Riley), 7, 9 (Andy Sacks), 11 (Tony Latham), 15 (David Ximeno Tajeda), 33 (Frank Siteman), 34 (Penny Tweedie), 42 (Chris Craymer); Wayland Picture Library *cover* (APM Studios), 8, 10 (APM Studios), 12, 13 (APM Studios), 14 (Context), 19, 20 (Context), 21 (Context), 22, 23, 25, 29 (APM Studios), 31, 36, 38 (Context), 39, 40 (Context), 41 (Context), 45 (APM Studios); Zefa 16, 17 (CH Gupton), 26, 43.

Index